Dedication

To every reader, patron, supporter, and fan; your support inspires and encourages me to continue along this journey and operate in my gifts and flow in my passion. Thank you for your enduring love.

To Princess Amira, God couldn't have chosen a sweeter, kinder, more loving child to bless we me. I am always so amazed by your gentleness and compassion towards others. Thank you for inspiring me with your love. **–Mommy**

I am ever mindful of my many blessings and I am grateful to God for such a loving, supportive, encouraging and patient husband, children, family and friends. **–TF**

This is for all the little artists with big imaginations, dreams, and stories. Keep reaching and sharing your work. Never give up, because you never know who's watching the world you're building. **-Racheal**

Published by Your Go2 Girls
Printed by Your Go2 Girls, USA
ISBN-13: 978-1519275967
ISBN-10: 151927596X
www.AmirasHeart.com

Text Copyright © Alitasha Fuller 2015   Illustrations © Alitasha Fuller

All rights reserved. No part of this publication may be reproduced or transmitted in any form or by any means of electronic, mechanical, digital, including photocopy, recording or any information storage and retrieval system without the written
permission of Alitasha Fuller.

For information regarding book signings, appearances, events or bulk purchases please email at Tasha@yourfabulousgo2girls.com

Mommy I Want To Be A Princess

Author: Tasha Fuller

Illustrator: Racheal Scotland

Published by Your Go2 Girls, Inc.

ISBN-13: 978-1519275967

ISBN-10: 151927596x

www.AmirasHeart.com

Mommy I want to be a Princess

Well a Princess you will be,
because that is what Amira really means.

No Mommy, I want to be a real Princess!

Well if you are going to be a Princess then Mommy must be a queen
and as ruler of this Kingdom I can grant every dream,
Kindness and compassion are things you already possess
So look into the mirror and let mommy do the rest.

If you want to be a Princess you must look the part
A crown, a gown and some ruby slippers to give you a little spark.

But looking like a Princess is only the start,
Being a real Princess is about what's in your heart.

Go down the castle stairs where your chariot awaits,
we don't want you to be late for your very important date.
Stepping into her chariot it was more than she had ever dreamed.
Lined with diamonds and gold it was really fit for a queen.

With the crack of the whip she started flying through the air
Flying so high she could see the entire kingdom from up there.

As she stared out her window surrounded by clouds
There was a bump and a rumble and then she hit the ground.
Tumbling out of her chariot with no help in sight.
Amira started to dance and sing to the animals delight.

"I want to be a Princess and a Princess I will be,
because that is what Amira really means.
My name is Amira and I have a special date
I must keep moving because I can't be late."

She walked through the forest wondering where everyone could be,
Then she stopped and she said, "someone is watching me!"
So she walked towards the bushes and she pushed back the leaves
and to Amira's surprise what did she see?

A little girl named Victoria hiding in the trees.
Amira reached out her hand and said, "Can I help you please?"
But Victoria just stood there with tears in her eyes
So Amira hugged her softly and whispered, "Please don't cry."

"I want to help you and I'll do my very best,
Just tell me the problem and I'll do the rest."
Victoria whispered quietly,
"I can't find my shoes and I have surely lost my way,
and without someones help, I will be here to stay."
"Don't worry Victoria,
my mommy taught me to always be prepared,
Take my ruby slippers, I have an extra pair."

So they danced and they sang as they went on their way,

"I want to be a Princess and a Princess I will be,
because that is what Amira really means.

My name is Amira and I have a special date.
I must keep moving because I can't be late.
So join me in this journey as I find my way
When I get to my destination we will surely play."

As they walked along and the trees began to clear
Amira heard a faint sound in her ear.
It wasn't a whisper or a whimper but something sounded wrong,
so she walked a little farther and listened a little harder,
then she heard this sad song.

"I was running and jumping and the rock tore my dress,
I can't go to the party because I look a mess."

Amira slowly approaches, making sure not to startle,
Then she softly says, "I have a dress you can borrow."
With a smile on her face and a sparkly new gown,
Karis graciously accepted the matching crown.
So the three walked on as Amira began to sing,

"I want to be a Princess and a Princess I will be,
because that is what Amira really means.
My name is Amira and I have a special date
I must keep moving because I can't be late.
So join me in this journey as I find my way
When I get to my destination we will surely play."

Then Amira noticed the sun began to set
She became a little sad because she hadn't reached her destination yet.
But off in the distance what did she see?
Amira whispered, "Is that really my chariot waiting for me?"

Swiftly they moved as she picked up the pace,
And with every step she thanked God for his grace.
Into the chariot they made a mad dash.
She hoped and prayed that she would be there in a flash.

But in a sad tone Amira sang her song.
"I want to be a Princess and a Princess I will be,
because that is what Amira really means.
My name is Amira and I have a special date
I must keep moving because I can't be late.
So join me in this journey as I find my way.
When we get to my destination we will surely play."

She stepped out the chariot with her head hung low.
She missed her special date and she really wanted to go.

"Did you enjoy being a Princess?" her mommy asked with a smile, Amira answered sadly,
"I didn't get to be a Princess because my chariot broke down."

Then mommy reminded Amira,
"Remember that gowns and crowns are only a part,
being a real Princess starts in your heart.
Kindness and compassion are what you shared today,
and the way you make people feel will never go away."

"Victoria has new slippers and Karis has a new gown,
Now with your acts of kindness you have earned your Princess Crown.
Amira is a princess and that's what you will always be
Treating people with kindness and compassion, that's what being a Princess really means."

Tasha Fuller

Tasha Fuller is coming off the overwhelming success of her first two children's books, **It's Bath Time Baby**, featuring her oldest daughter Aukema and, **Little Freddie's in a Zone**, starring her son and his love for all things sports. It was only a matter of time before her youngest daughter Amira would have her moment to shine. Tasha fulfills her daughter Amira's desire to be a "real" Princess with the release of **Mommy I want to be a Princess**.

Tasha, using both parenting and poetry, takes Amira on a whimsical journey to demonstrate the true meaning of being a Princess. Amira is presented with opportunities to build character along her journey and through kindness and compassion she finally understands that being a real Princess is not about the crowns and the gowns, but what's in your heart and how you make people feel.

Tasha, continuing to operate in her gifts and flow in her passion, is writing a book on marriage with her husband Freddie and preparing for the release of her fourth children's book, **Chores, Chores, Chores**.

Tasha currently resides in Virginia with her husband Freddie II and their three children Aukema, Freddie III and Amira.

Racheal Scotland

Racheal started drawing at a very young age. Art was always a hobby until she decided to continue her education in Visual Communications and Interior Design. Racheal taught herself how to draw digitally and works full time as an artist, specializing in portraits and character art.

Racheal finds inspiration from everyday life and moments from her childhood. Her style focuses on semi-realistic, fantastical, young women. Capturing a gentleness and emotion, but strength in the same breath.

Racheal resides in Chicago, Illinois.

All things are possible
if you believe !!

All things are possible if you believe it!

Made in the USA
Charleston, SC
04 May 2016